Separated
from the Sun

Separated
from the Sun

İlhan Sami Çomak

edited by
Caroline Stockford

Translated by
Canan Maraşlıgil, Öykü Tekten,
İdil Karacadağ, Sevda Akyüz,
Şakir Özüdoğru, Paula Darwish,
Clifford Endres and Caroline Stockford

STACK
BOOKS

Smokestack Books
1 Lake Terrace,
Grewelthorpe,
Ripon
HG4 3BU

info@smokestack-books.co.uk

www.smokestack-books.co.uk

ISBN 9781739772239

Smokestack Books
is represented
by Inpress Ltd

Contents

Foreword

Kurdish poet İlhan Sami Çomak is a remarkable man who has published nine books of poetry from within the confines of Turkey's highest security prison, the F-Type facility of Silivri, north of Istanbul. Despite the extreme privation of his surroundings and the stories of hardship and injustice he has heard from fellow inmates over his (to date) 28 years in prison, İlhan's poems are full of wonder at nature, love and communion. In the words of Turkish poet Haydar Ergülen, a champion of Çomak, 'İlhan has turned everything to poetry'. Although writing some works in Kurdish, İlhan writes mostly in his second language, Turkish.

Born in Karlıova, Bingöl in south-eastern Turkey in 1973, İlhan spent his childhood and youth in the countryside riding horses, herding goats and listening to his mother telling stories at night under their earth-roofed home. İlhan tells us in letters from prison that it is his imagination that has allowed him to endure and to write poetry in such harsh conditions and that he is grateful to his mother for having fed his imagination with Kurdish folk tales and songs when he was a child.

İlhan studied geography at Istanbul University. During his studies, in 1994, he was arrested at a cafe in Istanbul; swept up like so many other young Kurdish people following a military coup in the country and was taken to a torture centre. Following 19 days of heavy torture İlhan signed a false confession to say that he had lit forest fires in the name of the outlawed PKK (Kurdistan Workers' Party) near Istanbul. 'They beat me so badly that I still have the pain and scars on my shoulders,' he says. 'They even drove me up above Istanbul and made me pose between two soldiers with an empty petrol can. There are no forests there. It was all a lie.' He was just 22 years old. Despite the falsity of his confession, İlhan was sentenced to death by a State Security (military) court. His sentence was then commuted to life in prison: a total of 36 years.

In 2007 the European Court of Human Rights declared a mistrial and his case was scheduled for retrial. At this point İlhan should have been released to await a new series of hearings. Instead, he was kept in prison until the Supreme Court in Istanbul once more found him guilty of the alleged crime of 'separatism', and sentenced him, once again, to life in prison. The failure to release him following the ECtHR decision for retrial means that İlhan spent 22 years in pretrial detention.

During his imprisonment, İlhan began to write poetry, publishing his first book, *Gitmeler Çiçek Kurusu* (Going resembles dried flowers), in 2004. This was followed by *Açık Deniz* (Open sea) in 2007, *Günaydın Yeryüzü* (Good morning earth) in 2011, *Kedilerin Yazdığı İlahi* (Hymn composed by cats) in 2014, *Yağmur Dersleri* (Rain lessons) in 2017, *Dicle'nin Günlüğü* (Diary of the Tigris) in 2017 and *Bir Sabah Yürüdüm* (One morning I walked) in 2017.

In 2019 his eighth collection, *Geldim Sana* (I came to you) won the prestigious Sennur Sezer prize for poetry and in March 2022 his ninth volume of poetry, *Hayattayız Nihayet* (We're still alive), won the Metin Altıok prize for poetry. This was the prize that İlhan always wanted to win. Metin Altıok had been his teacher in primary school and was later to be one of 37 individuals, mostly Alevi intellectuals, who were murdered in an arson attack by a radical Islamic group on a hotel in Sivas in 1993. On hearing that he had won his late teacher's eponymous prize, İlhan said, 'It means so much to me. It feels as if my teacher has reached out his hand and patted me on the head; that he approves of my poetry.'

Since 2018, when we at PEN Norway began to campaign for İlhan, we have received and translated over 80 poems for İlhan from poets all around the world. A few of Ilhan's responses to their poems are included in this book. PEN Norway have shared news of İlhan via the website www.ilhancomak.com. İlhan is now an honorary member of Wales PEN Cymru, PEN Norway, Austrian PEN and Irish PEN na hÉireann. In March 2022 he received the Norwegian Authors' Union's Freedom of Expression Prize.

In order to communicate with İlhan we are assisted by the dynamic and irrepressible law lecturer and campaigner İpek Özel. İpek is İlhan's official visitor, his 'Mackenzie Friend' and it is hardly possible to account for our gratitude to her in transmitting so many poems back and forth over the years. İpek works tirelessly for him and for other students in prison; for İlhan is Turkey's longest-serving student prisoner.

In Turkey İlhan's case is well known and the campaign for his release has been going on, peaking every few years, since the early 2000s. The country's Supreme Court of Cassation ruled in 2021 to confirm his life sentence following the appeal and İlhan continues to live in solitary confinement in a huge and brutal prison complex with 23,000 other inmates. His release on parole is scheduled for June 2024.

At PEN Norway, and indeed in most PEN centres globally, we have a Writers in Prison Committee. We encourage our members and members of the public to write to poets and writers like İlhan. But some people struggle to comprehend what it is like to be locked up continually for decades.

It is the small anecdotes that drive home İlhan's situation, such as when he recounted in a letter that the guards opened his cell door to the tiny and bare concrete yard one hour early in March 2021. 'I heard them unlock the door much earlier in the morning, at 7.00 instead of 8.00', he said. 'And I was able to rush outside, look up, and see the sun rise for the first time in 27 years.'

In this excerpt from his poem 'Things that are not here' he lists what he is missing:

> 'There are no women of selflessness and beauty
> no possibility to stretch out on grass
> and test the constancy of sky.
> There is no candle, just as there is no lamp.
> No darkness. There is absolutely no darkness.
> ...
> Life, separated from the sun.
> There's no direction here.
> But there is a way out.
> Always, a way out.'

İlhan's poetry is positive and uplifting. It is set firmly in the natural world and is full of rivers, fruit, flowers, high meadows, wild animals, ethereal women and the concepts of love and freedom. He talks about 'the greatness of living' and the ongoing struggle with his 'conscious dark', claiming the futility of staring into the abyss, 'it just repeats'. Ivy's slow creep pervades poems as a metaphor for the interminable waiting he has been made to endure. His sequences about women are dreamlike. He hears the sound of a dress as it lands on the floor and keeps a lipstick-stained paper handkerchief close to him. 'In the palms of a sleeping woman this year, I got older before the sun'. Women are always present but ethereal.

Birds and the sky feature a lot in his work. His only companions during the past eight years of solitary confinement (he formerly shared a larger dorm) have been a number of budgerigars, one after another, whose feathers he collects, along with feathers that drift down into the concrete yard outside his cell.

'Why does the sky not love me?' he asks. 'I am friends with the memory of light'.

Although only allowed seven books at a time, and having to change cells sometimes at no notice, when guards come in at 6am and begin to throw his possessions around, İlhan works daily at his poetry, claiming, 'I think I have to work harder than poets on the outside'.

This selected works contains poems from seven of his books. The poems are translated by Canan Maraşlıgil, İdil Karacadağ, Öykü Tekten, Sevda Akyüz, Şakir Özüdoğru and Paula Darwish, Clifford Endres and Caroline Stockford. İlhan has dedicated poems to İpek Özel, to Michael Baron and also to Margaret Owen, campaigners who have stood by him for many years. Michael also commissioned the *Trafika Europe* poems and five others in this book to be translated.

Some of the lines in İlhan's poems seem to grow like fractals with one image birthing another in a long spiral. İlhan packs the poetry with images as if trying to bring the whole world of his youth in the countryside around Bingöl into his cell.

His work is lyrical and even if the lines appear simple syntactically in Turkish, it is the feeling and connection between images and impulses that is more difficult to convey in translation. He often makes use of devices such as the 'devrik cümle' or 'inverted sentence'. Translating this faithfully is almost a paradoxical adventure, as all sentences are inverted in Turkish, whereas English syntax is Subject/Object/Verb. It suffices therefore to invert the syntax in English, of course, but as with many works in Turkish, the incidence of the verb (also carrying suffixes of tense, person and place) at the end of the line (or several flowing lines) means that one is treated to a cascade of image-loaded phrases, one after the other, until one finally lands at the verb and discovers 'who did what, and when.'

All the translators have carried İlhan's poems over with a deftness that lifts up these powerful meditations on loss, incarceration, freedom, love and beauty.

The most remarkable thing about İlhan is his purity and the lightness of his poetry despite his horrific living conditions. He has a playful sense of humour, after all these years of deprivation, and is grateful to all poets and supporters who have written to him. He says, 'they make me feel as though I am more outside prison than inside, these days.'

With thanks to the translators, to project assistant Sevda Akyüz and to Hege Newth, Secretary General of PEN Norway, for their great energy and support; to PEN Norway member Eugene Schoulgin who has been a constant friend to İlhan.

We hope that you will enjoy İlhan's poetry in English and that he will soon be freed; that we may one day meet him in person and hear him read.

Caroline Stockford
Turkey Adviser, PEN Norway
Bristol, July 2022

A letter from İlhan Sami Çomak to the reader

When a person is tested by a great injustice and forced to spend most of their life in prison it is easy to lose faith in life and in humanity itself. It then becomes essential to regain faith in these things by developing a passionate pursuit that will inspire hope and turn one's face towards the future. For me, this pursuit was, and is, poetry.

If I have managed to bring the hubbub of the crowd, the endless possibilities of life, the never-fading colours of nature into my narrow cell by way of pursuing a passion that would not betray me, you must know that this creative act was poetry. Poetry, which lights up time and space.

Poetry has given me an insight into the good and evil within people. Poetry has instilled in me a feeling of a stubbornly bright future and reality. It has given me a very different life: not the one I've actually lived here, but the one I missed; the one I always long to be living.

Now, as my poems are being published in English they are faced with a different test. When one considers that English is one of the major global languages, this big step means that not only will I be reaching a wider and very different readership, but my writing will be put to a more stringent test and will be measured accordingly. I am excited, but that excitement is outweighed by happiness.

I would like you, the reader, to forget about my 29 years of imprisonment; to disregard these difficult conditions and obstacles, and simply to read the poems I have written. I'd like you to focus on the poems themselves; the power of poetry to endorse life and to acknowledge no walls. Poetry has a very strong heart and it brings life with it, wherever it enters. Please look for this in my poetry, for the heartbeats of life that will not be silenced. Poetry is what really matters, not the place where it was written. This is what I believe.

I would like to express my sincere gratitude to everyone, who has worked hard on this book, and who has in turn fed the fire of my great happiness and excitement. My gratitude goes to my publisher, but especially to the translators of the poems. I would also like to express my biggest thanks to PEN Norway. It is an inexpressible honour and privilege for me to be a member of the PEN Norway family.

İlhan Sami Comak
Silivri Prison, Istanbul
June 2022

I came to you, life

for Ipek Özel

And the tree's shade buckles,
birds give all they know to their wings.
The wind blows an ovation and from the sun
comes the need to touch.

It is these leaves language
and sweetness are addressing,
now that the time for transgression has come.
Yet, on the hillsides is always the grace of abstention.
Think of the river when you get a chance.
Flowing vein in water's books, the knot's wish to be untied.

I'm speaking of the sound of a few colours. By denying
summer, embrace the spring and with a few tired steps
forgive me. Forgive this trembling cloud.

I came to you with the pain of hands cracked by the mud
I came to you, saying let childhood climb the garden wall again.
I came to you with the art of breathing sleep into morning.

Don't pull down my garden wall.
Let the path fill with the soft shapes of leaves.
Let the road dream of being covered up in grass.

There is no city we need to reach. Everything is here.
Open the window. Open it as the horses whinny
in the wideness of the world. Open it without speaking

of the shortness of summer, the never-ending winter.
Open it, that sky reflect the hidden symbols of my mind.
I came to you saying, 'Open the door to the presence of
existence' as the sky stirs in its form.

I came to you saying, 'Open the door of becoming.
Open the door of existence, to me.'

translated by Caroline Stockford

This morning

I look at you in the morning
and cut back the weeping willow.
Buds grumble and thirst for growth.
I look at you, scatter my own ashes.
I go out, add suns to the sunlight, walk on seeds.
Creation crashes down on me, the fingertips
of silence lightly restore balance.

I am on the hillside, shoulder to shoulder
with the rain in the uprising smell of soil.
On the sidelines are some words left unsaid.
I leap into the mystery of prayer and
laugh a little, grab hold of the breadth
of the breeze – how high are the clouds!
Roots look to earth and I to you.
I comb my unkempt hair.

I make my mark at the furthest point away,
feel the resonance of pain, the flowing of mirror's
reflection. The night is naked, flames impatient
to shoot. I have a few breaths left. My body tires.
Ashes of sudden silence rise up
and creation crashes down on me.

translated by Caroline Stockford

It's for this reason

It's for this reason I slashed my face.
By placing the resonance of a letter
in the space between us and the sun.
Laugh! I said to the tired face of rebellion.
I'm reconciled with this matter, now.
You know, like drawing a sketch and then staring,
asking, is it an apple, pear or apricot?
Saying, it's a plum! in that tone that's almost warm:
the tone of a pause.

Blood's brotherhood was so far away and stoppered.
Blood that pours from all wounds and flows to me.
My skull splits from storing up night's every sound.
Hear me well, hear me now!
I, who am the love of all the flowers –
I'll cross the Nile, I'll cross the Arab sands,
If the Tigris and Euphrates detain me –
It's blood, you know, even taste has a name –
Write my name like an eye; as a watchman.

Because the going is poetry, prose is the road.
And I would be a brother to my father,
carrying pain on my body like an amulet.

translated by Caroline Stockford

Life does not lie

for Michael Baron

I am between the moon and the tide
between the whisper and the scream.
When I was a child, had still the script of a child,
when I was hostage to my mother's pomegranate smile,
when I looked from the window to the full light of the garden
watching the practical philosophy of hands plucking the fruit tree.
In those times when we still heard the sound of frogs
when women passed through my life, and the lake was blue
when I knew the value of blue. I understand
there is pain, too, on the steps of life.

On the day of existence the wind rose up to meet me
resistance, like dew on the grass met my feet
Ripe fires grew across my body, and doves –
my feelings were met by the rustle of their wings.
In spring's demeanour I hear the sounds of cleaning
I hear footsteps of plains and mountains and the law
of snow melting. Earth grows damp in my memory,
fruit ripens, stones' habitual weight grows light,
makes it to flow and tremble as it wishes.
In my place between trouble and wellbeing
I hear the song of happiness from the world.
As goodwill blossoms: Life does not lie! I say
it does not lie!

translated by Caroline Stockford

Let us not speak

Let us not speak so much, I say.
Let us laugh, leaping the fences of mistrust.
The wind is blowing, wind is blowing.

Let us whisper into each other's ears,
into your ears. In the river's secret places,
in the tender shade of rushes, in the composite of mudbricks

as the whole city sleeps, let us speak little in a corner
the light can't reach. There is belief between us
and the dryness of a thirsting mouth.

Let us sit, pour out the pictures
in our heads on the surface of the water.
Let us love the carnation as it says my confession is red.

Falcons fly to the world's most lonely height.
Let us open our windows to the fluid beauty of butterflies.
With the art of feeling let us hear the heart's rushing.

I will sing songs and throw stones, like I used to,
I will ride horses and recite poetry.

Here there is a depth and here, a fire.
Here lies a word, unspoken!
Let the doves coo, but let us not speak.

translated by Caroline Stockford

I have my reservations

Why does this sky not love me?
I cannot fly, I have my reservations,
I can't be bothered with myself,
am jumpy and the path is a void.
Huma bird, mythical Huma bird!
How well you resemble my sojourn here on earth.

My tears are like centipedes in the corridor,
Why, in my paintings' yellow mornings, in a wide impasse
in one of the host of unfrequented spaces in the east,
Why didn't you jam an olive branch into my mouth?
Why did you leave me dreaming of earthlands and rainbows?

Why, in the deluge of new places didn't you give me
completely to the magnificence of the mountains?
Huma bird, Huma bird!
How well you resemble my sojourn here on earth.

I have my reservations, I can't be bothered with myself
What does this sky want with me?
The rainwater stores turn purple, yellow.
Whilst approaching with love
and drinking wine to the joy of hushed moments.

I wrote the bottom of the well by letting the water weeds talk.
Oh you suns! I have grown lighter by abundance.
I know, of course, that distances have been memorised
by way of my white, my brilliant white feathers.

On my breast are sidelong glances,
The tinder is in my chest, trees crackling, I feel you burn:
I, the Huma bird, never lands on the plains of your loins.
Like stunned and cageless animals
We live on water's other shore.

translated by Caroline Stockford

Things that are not here

There are no kids scaling back walls
to skip school. No human bond of good
making friendship from mere words.
There are no stones for throwing stones
No flowers pooling dew, no rivers
overflowing the map. No fresh-baked
smell of sesame bread to summon up
a crowd. There are no women
of selflessness and beauty, no possibility
to stretch out on grass and test the
constancy of sky. There is no candle,
just as there is no lamp. No darkness.
There is absolutely no darkness.

There are no turnings of the seasons,
no eclipses of the moon. No earth,
no plants in their simple elegance.
No cat's paws, no sweat-drenched
headlong of a horse. No curtain
for breeze to life, no mouldering
bunches of grapes.

Life; separated from the sun.
There's no direction here.
But there is a way out.
Always a way out.

translated by Caroline Stockford

You decide

But whenever I think of myself
you appear by my side in the form of a silence
We swallow the light.
A rose garden, think of it, in the middle of the desert.
You touch that place with your wound,
The desert softens somewhat.
At that moment, right at that moment
Like taking a copper tray, hanging it on the wall
you think of me with fresh new eyes, love me.
You create me anew.
Should we name this thing? You decide.
But whenever an alarm clock goes off
here and there in places that I cannot hear,
you become a ringing thing,
Like a nun thinking of renewing her vows,
you say 'Welcome' to the greatness of living.
You give form to water.
Is this what they call surface tension?
With a strange love you open your mouth,
might regret that some things don't work out.
With these eyes that come from
when you first began to love me –
their depth, the burden of meaning –
With these things I say, 'Love me'.

translated by Caroline Stockford

Feather collecting

With my conscious dark I correct my writing.
Why did I clap and come into this world? Hear me.
I asked the world whilst in your presence: Why did I land?
These days my mind is seeded with flight.
Not with the static stare of stone, but degree by degree
with a flight that denies the road. With boundlessness
that opens the woven cage of sky: frighten me
Prove me the stars' slightest movement!

My consciousness I refresh in the darkness,
bird feathers I collect for you. At the sound of wings
the pomegranate cracks. From the hoop that is love
to the palm of the leaf. I came from the stratum of rain
in the conscious-raising roar. I drank water.
From this stairway of no sound and into the world
why did I come? I sing songs with the distant dream
of flying. My name suits well to blue,
and your name fits the distances.

The wind blows, the wind is blowing, shadows leaning.
I collect up the blowing, the footstep sounds of morning,
the clear destiny of laughing to your heart's content.
Yes, in this realm of sheer habit why did life come to me?
The limitless law of flight is steeping in your warmth.
The lightness of embracing my awareness refreshes.

What meaning has flying?
I have bird feathers, I have the sky,
a heartbeat that is washed by your laughter –
I have this.

translated by Caroline Stockford

I left you behind me

I walked, left you behind me
The candle was burning and I gave up melting
I came and listened to songs of *Zeki Müren*
and more by *Sezen Aksu* and even more
I listened to the things I cannot hear
Listened to all sounds, read all the books
I looked at the sky and filled pages with my writing
Out I went and looked at myself, gilding the mirrors
I knocked on doors, ate sour apples
I walked, left you behind me but caught your breath
Glanced at the so-called unreadable newspapers
        I tested my eyes
Placated the waters, for a few moments went
        silent
Grew cold, I turned to the moth that stays out of the light
It inspected my palms, my hands and my eyes
'You see,' I said, 'that's why I gave up crying.'
I walked, left you behind me
Thought of the sun and women I've loved
I whistled, woke everyone, woke everyone up
        I *so* woke them up
I counted all numbers, took leave of the bad ones
The roads became lively, I walked, left you behind me.

It's flowing, life, how nicely it flows!
I walked. Left you behind me.

translated by Caroline Stockford

Life is seeing the flight of a butterfly

for Margaret Owen

I am water's tradition, surrounded by ill will in this world
I keep the taste of people's mouths, take their pulse.
I pass over lands that are nipped at by tiredness
A Londoner, I know not where this links of the chain will join
No cage can contain the colours of my heart, and my breath –
I know not in which sky it finds voice.

A Londoner, but when the sparrows lay their eggs
when children go hungry and fish are left breathless.
It's as if this means nothing, those left behind mean nothing.
Wind and flowers call me with the reconciled voice of loneliness.
Life is the breeze, the cool place where dew meets plants.
The red bag of the rains drags with my every step
         and I repeat to myself
'Life is about walking without thinking where you're stepping.'

I am friends with the memory of light, with apricot's kernel
with the solidity of stone inscribing my book with the will
of the waves the stillness of the sea. My mind is filled with questions
and the insistence of migrating birds I repeat to myself
life is seeing a butterfly land and then fly
life is gauging the pace of the Thames in your mind!

translated by Caroline Stockford

Ilhan's response to John Macker

You rightly say I've stayed so long in exile
in this well, the sun, never returning!
I still have a yearning within me for light.
I love the sun, and the loop of the moon
I see so little of. Each spring the steam
files up from warming soil. I'm as far from spring,
soil and steam as a severed hand.

Still I piece all that I miss into a single picture.
Into that wounded bird called freedom.
I must do it, so I won't forget.
Life is severe, defiant and all walled
because I'm here. I say: the blossoms
of the first cherry tree, breaking into air,
How do they smell? Can you tell me this
and what their colour is?
I seem to have forgotten.

translated by Caroline Stockford

Ilhan's response to Blas Falconer

I have a need for levity
for balloons that quiver and expand, that take
from me the heavy burden of life; of time.
Like the line of the register, I need lightness
like the resilience of fruit pips,
the silent passing that reaps all seasons,
strength of labourers' calloused hands,
the distance at which men and women
walk together, protecting the fresh,
new feelings of beginnings.

I need the unquestionable survival of trees,
will of starlings to shoal the sky
and the lightness this lends to me.
This, when my journey is heavier than heavy,
stretching longer and longer,
I tell myself to believe in magic,
even if it's short or fleeting.

Like, when clouds trail up and off,
I stare at their feet and that joy of blue
until my whole self takes sides with beauty.
And ask, should I favour being filled
with love's radiant pomegranate?
Say what you will, I'm ready to believe.

translated by Caroline Stockford

Ilhan's response to Menna Elfyn

I give praise to the embraces of women
that reach right into my cell.
I give praise to the wind's own knowing
that it is wind. I am without a door yet my wings
splay wide as an atlas. Birds love me.
I hear that delight in their songs
and the quiet of these blues and greens
gives me peace. There is a stairway
that leads to the very height of life.

I love the birds because we're brothers in hunger,
as the window creaks with tiredness in its frame.
So then sing your song, beautiful bird.
Let us go blazing to the seas, to my childhood,
when I believed in all the stories, to the times when
I fell and fell, grazing my knees,
to the pain of my hand when it would bleed.
To the wound of the skies and the earth.
To the pure, bright experiment of rain.
I am with the birds.
Life accepts me again.

translated by Caroline Stockford

Ilhan's response to Alice Oswald

And I'd hidden in my dreams the cooing doves.
I sought the tired trees and your hands
in my body's harmony with another.
Hid unguarded smiles of flowers from the wrath of the wind.

In the beginning, I said it was *endless*. The crucifix of the desert
entered time's eyes, slipped, knowing the ruggedness of earth,
slipped, breaking the mirror of existence and nothing.
Fright took form in my body, came and sat in life's voice.
Were I to scream, my mouth would but summon the void!

For there is a weight that holds the soul to objects,
grace that carries seeds to far off places.
The fresh white of a cloud, desire inclining us to flight,
the lightness of scentless rain and snow and more, and more
things that give soul to our souls.

We're one, with all objects, just so!

translated by Caroline Stockford

Ilhan's response to Jeffrey Cyphers Wright

Before looking to that clean corner of shade and budding lilac
I washed my face and hands with copious water.

Now, so refreshed. Resolute as a drop on the rim of a glass,
in its will to find ground.

Taken in by your words I passed a time or two, following you:
How good that I did.

In case there is no rock, let the East Wind take refuge in my body
May it shelter in the ringing of our voices as we sing songs by
moonlight.

And don't forget, please don't forget: the outstretched hand of the
river accompanies us too. In meadow's taste is knowledge of far
distant places.

I saved myself from stumbling before, and will, once more,
And yet 'the weight of the world is love', is love, is love.

My fears are all within me, my freedom too.
Barren minds weigh down dark night and the devotion of moonlight.

Light one more candle, please.
A candle to accompany the weight of the world.

Let us protect the trembling flame.

translated by Caroline Stockford

Ilhan's response to Lee Herrick

We had a celebrated pasture, that stroked
my child's head with tenderness. We called it
'Tapë Kozikan' in Kurdish: Peak of Trenches.
It took its name with Russian occupation, pre-WWI.
I saw no trenches, just empty, bleached-out cartridges.
I took its name to heart, like an old memory.

On Tapë Kozikan I rode my first horse. A chestnut.
Accepting me, thanks to its biddable breeding.
Bareback, I gripped its mane, its bright skin swarmed
my legs like a warm wave. The horse's power made itself known,
and I suffused the Spring with laughter.

His name was Koçe, he smelled clean, like someone
from the same house. I had no fear. Do we learn it retrospectively?
So I say: The horses that sweat and gallop in my poems
all assume the shape of Koçe.

Your poem filled the void of my lost past with a fresh breath.
Poetry is on the side of the weak, a nameless bud,
giving height to those who wish to fly. One day,
let's walk at Tapë Kozikan with the joy of children
playing hide-and-seek. Let's walk, walk, walk,
until we smell the lofty scent of a horse.

You ride on the horse with your tiredness
and your words, and I will hold the halter.
Friendship like that is such a thing!

translated by Caroline Stockford

Ilhan's response to John Casquerelli

I place my notebook before me,
and life expands exponentially!
But I long for the forests: geometry of green
I want the other side of light and dark;
other side of the cool of morning.
Sometimes I think of the stream,
bathing in waters I thought were all mine,
in childlike excitement,

Opening my arms in those wingless days
pretending to be a bird! Immeasurable heat
of the sun mixed with plenteous thunder of rain.
I stop and listen to the dripping tap, listen
to seedlings as they pierce earth. Yes, I listen
to the tedious onrush of time with tears
for my memories! All that's denied to me
calls to earth and in the name of longing.

Laughing and crying I stretch a hand, for ever,
to all colours, fragile as a stemless rose.
Yes, hunger is a beast of all seasons
But love is everywhere!

translated by Caroline Stockford

What good is reading poetry?

It's good for making hands fine enough to touch silk
and for feeling the moment that stone turns impatient

It's good for looking in the eyes of hungry cats
and extending curiosity out among all animals

It is the darkness that makes my night voice heard
and makes it easier to say 'the moon will come up late'

For years my feet have been cold, so cold.
When I say this, it helps me compare winter to snow

Spring will begin today, I know.
Reading poetry helps me believe that feeling

It reminds me I don't miss the Istanbul bustle,
lets me know things to tell my love in a letter

When I'm tired, to stop and rest, not to drink water when I sweat,
it helps me to cry and fret over wildfires, over death

To know anger's reserved just for evil,
to stop and ask forgiveness of women

To feel youth when young, to understand it later on,
It's good for helping me to sit and write new poems

Good for helping me seduce and flatter
then to kiss my love when the leaves turn yellow

translated by Caroline Stockford

We are after you

We are in the time of leaves, in the evening
          of sprinkling salt
The whirlpool is expanding on end, troubles multiply
Heat of stones walks from the past to the future
We are in search of smiles infusing light
          with the dried fruits and nuts in our pockets
The sky slits open by the crackling sound of branches
Maybe here at our feet
with our steely gaze parsing the marble
with the spirit of a horse going down to the water
we are after the wind

translated by Öykü Tekten

In the beginning

In the beginning, I sat down to look at the sky
The leaves falling and the day humid
Someone came and took away the words from my mind
Someone came and built a fire out of hay
Darkness is night's quality – I became
        worthy of darkness
I drew a face onto the day with the chains of reality made from light
        the cloud was astonished
I reached out for the morning with the solitude's pomegranate in
        the garden
I perspired once again and the horizon expanded
Each direction I looked deepened
The meaning marched into my eyes.

I settled inside the lines by reading time and again
My mind was familiar with the sounds of leaves, the candid
        body of letters
All of a sudden, I sought peace. There was a plethora of meaning
I denied the falling of snow, the waves of the sea,
        the proliferation of life
They took me away from my own words, tension of the bow,
intense solitude of the sycamore, and my thirst
        the moment I reached the water.
I was poisoned by reason.

translated by Öykü Tekten

Partial look

In my dreams, I always have a partial look at life
The clothes hanging in the balcony cast a shadow onto my picture
I love the night. I am the only one understanding
        the waters stirred up by the wind
I say the sun, the sun the most, as an extinct barefoot

There are also rivers here that deepen by overflowing
My mind has been hiding from me for some time
Time is looking with distant and faint sounds

I am ready to walk. I recognized the pigeon by its cooing
        What I know about the stars doesn't add up to sleep
Because I find my name strange with the signals from the sea
The mountains intensify the frostbite
        My word is about the melting of stone
the look of a horse at a horse
And yet the well's coolness melts in the void
Time is always getting ready for eternity

translated by Öykü Tekten

Bond

There is agony in my voice that women know
I am angry. My throat is parched.
I am carving myself out to fit into the day
This is my job. This is life. And I come down to the
                          the street with freezing darkness
Needles knit my paleness, the shadow goes
                          toward the sea
Tuning of the night rusts silently
A jaded pulse everywhere
And yet I have my bond with life.

Thunder in the sky, the leaf changes colours
The chirps gather on the curtain of a hushed dawn
My face twitches with the depiction of astonishment
There is something on the wall, hard and unfit
                          for the desert
Perhaps there is rain that doesn't blend with water nearby
                          perhaps on the rocks

The stone I turn to over and over again
suffocates me with its heavy consciousness,
                          my arms are exhausted
My sentence expands with uncertainty of mist
And yet I have a solid bond with life
                          quite solid.

translated by Öykü Tekten

Such is life

Now you say 'photograph'
and I say 'photo' in short, quite short
Sometimes it is replaced by picture
and everyone knows what that means
You say 'metro' and talk about
                    taking it politely
I add the bus as if extending it like a line
It is not only a line, but a tumult, crowded
                    rough and tumble
From my own experience I know life is hard
So is the sea and the mountain. Everyone knows this
from what the wave and the wind
from what the rain and the snow
                    bring
Such is life.

With the heart's rhythm the heat passes through the body
The chills settle into the most secluded utterances of memory
Time walks slowly over pomegranate seeds
When water meets water, the parched soil hums
                    in a broken way
No one knows what the mountain tells the stone
The dew migrates toward the sunrise
                    as always
The mind is filled with the names of trees and flowers
and yet still withers. Perhaps this memorization is because
                    of withering and shedding leaves

In short, quite short, you should take photographs
since the photo and the picture replace each other
Hop on the bus, both forget and don't about being polite
The hardship of life is included in life. Yes, such is life.
Don't forget.

translated by Öykü Tekten

Tilt

I first think of darkness
then what overflows of you
with the colour of frothing milk

Your body has a tilt
an uninterrupted bond between your dream and reality
I am afraid the mist never disperses,
from distances everything takes its shape

A pristine smoke rises
                  to my eye level
I renew my bond with life all the time
and shake off my writing. Everything is quite clear.

My mind is always rolling down to your chest.

translated by Öykü Tekten

I knew it as such

The dark side of the mountains
was a colour jealous of blue, I knew it as such
Like a clumsy rock, I split the air into two
I whistled
I likened whistling to horses
With a slice of bread whose face gives meaning to heat
Among all kinds of smells
the breath of silence breaks the waves
at the first illusion devoted to water and stone
I knew it as much as rain and suns
Then I turned my head
with knots tied all wrong
I harmonized the images of moss.
At the back, a woman was braiding her hair
I saw seas inside those braids
and constant waves
in the middle of her mouth

translated by Öykü Tekten

Earth-roofed home

I am in our earth-roofed home
fire burning in the hearth

Has anyone seen the first blaze of youth slip away?
Has anyone heard, in the night resounding with frog calls, the
owl's hoot steeping in the dark?

I am afraid!
No doubt, the wind embodies my fear as does the sound of
pebbles rattling.

I am afraid! Alone and chasing smells
coming from the orchard.
The moon is in the sky. My moon.

And on earth, the silence of sleep.

translated by Şakir Özüdoğru

Rise, oh sea!

Not long now till I reunite with the life I call openness.
My foot has a wish from me: To print it on sand

without socks and naked, size 42.
Seven o'clock. It is exactly seven o'clock.
Indeed, I can see the sky.

The moon has a body. I am measuring
the white flight of clouds.
Rise, oh sea! Waves, where are you?
Not long now till life, the dream I call openness.

I should put my faith in that!

translated by Şakir Özüdoğru

Infinite desert

You know how by the side of the road
Between the brambles, a seed
That's the best name for it, a seed
Drops, foiling solitude, to alight
before life, infusing in earth.

What was it he said about this, Jesus of the Nazarenes? Anyway,
hold my hand!
As the rain scatters,
Over the curtain airing gracefully in the infinite desert
Yes, there, the sound of time tolls in our bodies

What was it she said about this, Mary Magdalene? Anyway, Kiss me!
We are the wind!

translated by Paula Darwish

Say I want now

My brunette, the blessed star of my patience
I got bloodshot eyes
Like I willed the snow into melting
Like sleep was on my side and the bottom of the sea
The notebook of sorrow touches my lips
It is written crossed out erased by your fingers
As much as you love me, scare me with your compassion
As much as you undress and kiss me
As you ebb and flow
Let your secrets touch me inside

Say I want now the night to look like
a man lying on the sidewalk.
I say I wish when I was in school
the women I loved holding lilac blue times
early in the morning wind
embroidered me on their handkerchiefs as solitude.

Now with your smile opening like a rose in my palm
seasons kiss and smell my forehead
I know what follows
and how a river flows to become a river
Because I stopped to catch my breath facing the mountains
the twist of the knife ceased as well
What with the sun sweat and worries
You appeared in my gardens next
And we opened up.

translated by Sevda Akyüz

Happy birth

Forty loaves of bread, thirty-four drops –
Not wine, it is water –
After eating and drinking,
I surmounted the stone
looked for sand looked for sand
a grain of sand that would get in my eye
Then, you know, I went along with silence
leaving behind another year

I suddenly grew up and descended to your presence
I thought of my hands, the sun is about to age
And I liken the sound of rain to the water I drink
This year snow is a certainty
in the palms of a sleeping woman,
This year I aged before the sun did
My heart was the distance.

translated by Sevda Akyüz

Pondering

Yesterday there was light here. Today as well.
And I passed through the sky with my arms and earth with
my feet

I pondered over breadcrumbs
added them to events
I donated the past to sleep
The ground was slippery and women smiled at a mirage
When the shadow trembled the silence broke.
Plains went up the mountain.
Time was flat.
Everything in the book walked to that flat plane.

I am recording the smell of fresh bread on paper
The mulberry tree whispers from a sunny place
A tranquil rhyme emanates from the seclusion of silk
I beg for the sound of running water
and work my pen for the depth of the earth and sleep of the sea.
Both presence and absence transform me.
I pondered and the waves stopped, the mountain coughed.
A blabbermouth sky curled up into silence.
I pondered.
Life is something in curls.

translated by Sevda Akyüz

Before it is too late

I have rubbed my hands with the curves of your letters
I found 10 and 15 beautiful, because they were
those songs breathed out of this era
And now you, so happy, diving deep down
into the sea, wet
You will miss Diyarbakır when Bingöl will leave us
to grow again with each earthquake

I am a tall man they saw me
striding out of my non-existing spite
Pheasants, falcons, flies defy our skies
As a dark June lays on our embrace
Now I commiserate over our dying fires, the bronze
on the battlements of our tents.
Birds will fly
even if I shout.

For a while and a long line of letters: M, E, D, I and A
Your tiny hands your tiny mouth your tiny feet
Were the alphabet I never stopped learning by heart
And we...
(...)
On the mattresses of the sea wobbling
towards the windowless walls of Diyarbakır
And we
made love with the most eminent letters

translated by Canan Maraşlıgil

It began

Then we began with the light's subtle wit
Then the sky began with its briskest blue
In the waters where we were delayed
Carved time began. The mountain
Lacking majesty resisted with a knife's excitement
With sweat dripping into the night from a horses' pillion
The deserted valleys and the charming owls in the air
Began with brand new curves. Then the armies
With their cattle. Then the muezzin with his horrendously
Strong voice piercing our ears.
The tall cranes, the coin of the realm
The crescent cavalry of that era which passed through
This road began. Standing up with a Qur'an, one by one
All prophets began.
The sherbets we drank with our past loves
Our pens preceding our cut hands

We are growing up sobbing
Oh sea!
Then our sandal caught fire in the phosphorescence
Fishes swam up to breathe in the salty air
Death began
And where I said it began inside soap bubbles
Slippery daytime became tomorrow
It began with the voices coming from our lukewarm blood
In the sadness of dawn our faces began to turn to silt
Following the most tired question
Staying in our minds with a clicking clock
All the answers coming with the light began.

And so into the heart of the city
With a wicked smile
Wrapping anger on the light of their pupils
A lifetime began.

translated by Canan Maraşlıgil

Bingöl

Bingöl, the evening grows all day long
Bingöl, a dark and lonely salute goes out on the street
Bingöl, holds my hand with its open wound
Bingöl, the voice of Sheikh Said got entangled into his turban,
It still resonates,
Bingöl, we are going to the market under a tense sky,
To buy blue things
Bingöl, distance meanders towards Murat it meanders
Bingöl, we have no train no station, we come quickly
This time hey!
Bingöl, I lost my marbles, oh kid good luck to whomever
Finds them!
Bingöl, the sun keeps tiring us, I miss you very much
Bingöl, I swam until there's no more water in the lake,
Undress and hold me
Bingöl, with the stones' long words ask and ask about me
Love me before the Bridge
Bingöl, your light and your name suit us well, my hair is very curly
Bingöl, it is late, I am slowly advancing towards your feet
Bingöl, suddenly with the sound of shadow I am pulling away
From the wind
Bingöl, my pillow and my blanket are nicely flying towards you
Bingöl, 'And' I am starting by pouring fire
Into the womb of the earth
Bingöl, with the sword of nothingness the revenge of the abyss
Quenches our souls with its cut veins

Bingöl, provoking abundance with its purple hyacinths I
　　whistle
Bingöl, staying for the whirling dervishes, I write a note for
　　history
With a feather, trembling and aching:
Bingöl, Bingöl, why have you forsaken me!

translated by Canan Maraşlıgil

If I cry

I talk patiently
My body turning to the crying tigers in the licking waters
In the shadows of the gardens I withhold the winters
Against fortune's wheel
I understand that I knew as I was thinning the rain down
On my chest:
Turns out the mirrors I broke yesterday were fake
Because my bosom bleeds on the knees of autumn
The clouds biting my childhood's heart, bruise me
In reality I am part of the earth
My fists are the darkness of its few corners

I secretly stride through the sky's altar
Your solitude trails behind my whistle
The blooming noise flagellate my mouth
Fences have already surrounded my face
If I cry it is to test life
Yes, I keep chewing on my cheeks
With my tongue feeding the rose with new scents
I've made a token out of the circle of fear
Stretching the mornings towards the flow of water
The world's scythe has cut the power inside my lungs
I'm certainly tall because they passed me under a donkey
I walk, days are cooling down that moment
Mountains cleanse on my lips, the stars
Resemble my being cold.
The pocket knife that fell in the water when I jumped
Grows with my name that I had carved on trees
Because my bosom bleeds on the knees of autumn.

translated by Canan Maraşlıgil

Sleepless

I was sleepless
I was still seeking sleep when morning came
I chased the night it resembled a pine tree
I saw bread on the road and sweated
I saw the wind and a flower it was so beautiful oh my oh my
A bird was flying I also saw it
I've seen everything but sleep was nowhere to be found
Then I've seen the core
Next to the core I've looked at the corner of my heart
On the corner I was surprised to find my beloved sitting
I thought, go into the core of my heart, you will fall
So she found her place right in the core of my heart
But when there's no sleep love too is tiring, don't ask
I think love feeds insomnia
How general a statement about vicious circles.

I couldn't go on like this and lay down on the cracks
I can't find sleep, I can't
Helpless I turned to my love
With my voice I adorned the walls of my heart
Not a sound, she's asleep. There at the core
This moment I named: cruelty.
I looked everywhere. The North was missing
It must have left with her.

translated by Canan Maraşlıgil

Thinking of you

Do you know what's on my mind for you?
A mountain. Not only a mountain, its whisper
A whisper that brightens and multiplies with the zeal of stars
The immobile whisper of a shadow that started a journey
The whisper of the fire of worry pouring into my heart
The whisper of a misty bed and warming mornings
The whisper of our bodies standing in flames
In their silent idleness.
In my mind is the heavy weight of memories
The deep scents exuding from lush forests
Touching sleep we handed over to the rain
Leaking into the mirrors let it flow. The wire of existence is
    strained
Fingers touching the notes I know less
Clustered memories are squeezing by forgetting.
In my mind is the roof of night and day
Every name of the sun every name of darkness is in my mind
The wet face of clouds pouring itself out of shapelessness
Gives taste to the tongue through the cracking lip
Do you hear the owl's cry?
In my mind the owl is perched on the branch.
The sky wanders door to door with its fear of solitude
The wings of little Joseph bear midday's heat
On my mind is the fountain
Of drying distance, dew, plants and love.
Windows breathe looking at the garden
Water trembles from a lack of fish in the lake.
It is the knowledge of the wind that hurls the ash
It is the law of the moon that wakes you up in startle
Dreams bleed leaves fall, the stone's fate changes shell
The heavy look of time rises in my mind
I think of you...

translated by Canan Maraşlıgil

Frontward

And I woke against walls
Today is going to be a beautiful day afterwards
And the slanted-eyed women of the tents
The fishes caught in our nets
Like a tongue beating my mouth from their long caravans
They kept saying yes to all
Get up. Something bursts out of my big steps
Beautiful and castellated, from the feet of long and wet rose

And we walk in the burning hours
Only water draws out. Get up, I say, you time of times!
Migration is over! Your mouths clinging on the walls of the sun
The world must have reached its destination.
And I would wait there to collect the words of enlightenment
You know how a mountain grows out of the sea
I am kissing a woman from Diyarbakır on
Frontward seems so nice.

And our horses are sent to the world
The courtyard gets partly illuminated in the morning under
their hooves
I will come if you want
I would go to the plains where the sun remembers you
I will learn the fields, the pugnacious farm labourers by heart
If I return I must find you in the world's skirts
Be luminous, be beautiful, frontward.

translated by Canan Maraşlıgil

No room in my mind

If there's a room in life it is for separation
It isn't easy to claim, 'let's do it again', my love
Just like there is no water in that cloud
The falling leaf, the sleepy state of days
Children believing in fairy tales
Humming that song again...
If there's room in a life, my love
It is to love again.

So maybe it is definitely why
The last words will pass through my life
Love will pass, domes will rotate
Salt will get to the wounds through my blood
And it will pass that unforgettable promise, your eyes will pass
Death will reduce the seasons
Summer winter spring fall will all pass without you.

You are far ocean you are
Suspicion and intention are proof for love
My blood's harsh desires are petrified
And there's no room for happenstance
No room in my mind for separation
Even if you resemble other seasons there is no room
With your image I leak into the depths of time
My rose my dear rose my Songül
My sadness flat
One loneliness too many because of me.

translated by Canan Maraşlıgil

Rain lessons

At last the pigeons came to land on my tongue
We realised this in gratitude. In the dead-ends
of my chest I hid the coarse teeth of the morning
And the deserts walked to the sand's tom-toms
My mouth astonished entire and my mouth a master
And I am adding myself to you I am singing songs
Taking wing toward the bottom of some rain
Your long and flickering hair like the words
Touching my skin I dry out in foamy waves
Rising to the sea's long sentences
Memorise those stones think of me long and slow
Towards the curling feet of rivers
I said come here you towards my being
Close the windows, the door, come.
I said I am counting to ten
Pass those lights, flourishing your skirt
Disrupt the night's spelling with ancient words
Towards my being, touching my being, I said come

The rain began to fall. I said keep dry. The swinging of
Your tresses will bring the gypsies out. Your hair
Carries the coolness of wet courtyards.
I said those kids are putting up their fingers
To your sunburnt skin, to life.
Cut the apple in half, quit smoking
Don't step on the poppies. I said look ahead
To the severed veins of my heart in clumsy waters
Surrounded by fog, with fortune-telling eyes piercing
And wild, with your restless mastery
Tried, with my shyness chilled, as a timid
Beautiful woman, look.

Your fairies suddenly rise within the battles in my mouth
With thin branches I test time towards the moon.
Extend my possibility. I said love, I said gently
I said say scorched, say morning to the dreams
Of the body we can never run out of forgetting
(The rain will become sleepy). Say a stone
With the gentlest love talk of what death knows
With astonishment write in your book my beard my hair
The mountain, spell them out, understand time, the tree.
Say I have crossed the bridges one by one the rivers one by one
I memorised the clouds in your accent.
And I want dresses in ant-sized steps
And the motion of redness kneaded in the dark
With sharp breath like knives inclined towards skin
You İlhan, you know the howness of this, from Bingöl
To Genç run the depth of the valley over my legs.
Give my life to the desert wilderness, to the bird
To the darkness. From the roots of my hair to the roof
Of the sky, extend the atlas of silence over your mouth
Parting in butterflies of silence.
I got on a horse and made towards the rain.
And I fell to your bosom with the seal of faulty calculations
I fortified the name of the night with the whims of dawn
In the distance, in the iron blaze of your name you my dear
Weave darkest rains smelling of the sea. (And if anything remains
Our horses with time-tearing face, heartfelt in their
Bridles, their speed a gift to solitary divans, will remain)
I have long since placed tall women's millstones
Over the seasons of my chest. Say rise up, say deserted
The fault-lines of the sun, beat whatever my tongue says
With the turbulence of those songs those rivers.
A city will come to mind, the turmoil of the city...
Say, my mind, say your clear bright days are cracking
Through your lips moving towards mine. Bend your knees
Good morning! The water's eagerness to disperse
Good morning! The weed yellowed in the steppe, say.
I got on my horse and came to you.

I brought rain to you with the rustling of beauty
Today starting from my brother's hands towards
His neck I kissed all your children.
What the droplet teaches: In love, you must become a torrent.
With the verses of your voice, say flood, say nonsense
Say enough with the wing-seeking blood
Of the birds we aim at with our slings.
If you come, the rains must come.
And some sun is constantly scraping our faces
With henna and partridges lotuses scrape our belatedness
Say, don't you keep whining, greet the dawn
Towards the soil's face. Shiver like wet birds
Bettered by dictionaries of love, come.

Don't cry with the dark face of the sea
Because this beauty overwhelms me
The cloud's bowed heads overshadow
The cracks among words with the heaviness of anger.
Say remedy, say the footsteps of distracted passengers
Towards the womb of fire. And bats repeat the darkness.
I would like to love you. I would like to become familiar
With cliffs, be hunted by bullets thirsty for my forehead.
Say it's true, say I have studied you like earthquakes
Dive down with the seeds of rain the particles of air
In my mouth, on my tongue, in the words of children.
And your breath bends towards the water. The birds'
Vast horizon trembles. Arise my rose, love my rose.
This blade will yet work more of the sea.

translated by İdil Karacadağ

Dreams of ivy

I whistle as I pass through silent nights
Impossible boredom in the air. Who knows
      whose boredom this is
In the pine grove a sparrow dreams of ivy.
Sometimes I write to dream. In my sleep
sometimes I write to wash. In the water
I circle books with squeaky-clean words. Incidentally
today is the eighteenth of July. The year
two thousand and twenty. The exact time, morning. Nine.
I want to touch the wind,
      the substance behind the rain.
I dropped my glass. Sound of splash
and leaf of crash enter my day.
Sometimes I write to a rose. I'm in all the colours.
No smell should be jealous!

translated by Sevda Akyüz, edited by Clifford Endres

Page of kindness

Almost turn of the season now. Ripeness
beckons. Maturity. Dominion of yellowed leaves
        not frippery.
I see people from where life cautions
houses where rough words multiply
        where joy fades from eyes.
Yet pomegranates are everywhere. Yes, we multiply
when we love. Surely the snow
will melt and run into the dry creeks
Freshness brought by melting in the moonlight
Let the breeze with soft fingers smooth the rough
Let us open the book on a page of kindness
as the lines on our palms merge into the light of colour.
Rejoicing fits us!

translated by Sevda Akyüz and edited by Clifford Endres

Kiss in freedom

Pretty things, nice things, things that pass through me
Towards the lowland, leafy things call out to me
From your hand on my forehead, naked testament
to solitude blooming in you and other things, I sit
and look at the wind sweeping away dust and hashish
I look at the wind and miss those lullabies
inducing sleep. Then all at once I'm thirsty
All at once I'm expecting crowds
in you, tolerance spreading through
the softness of your wet combed hair. Today
I woke up early for you, idle with the transparent
grandeur of dew, always straddling the border
of the hot breath of memory, things
that appear in far-off valleys and things
that kiss freely, a widening spectrum of colour,
wood smoke and solid darkness following the moon,
the hard veins in marble, things I always gather in you.

– If life must crack my mirror, let it be with you!

translated by Sevda Akyüz and edited by Clifford Endres

Perhaps you touch

I set fire to the maps and line up superlatives for you,
in fact I'm thinking of the rain, the chance that the sun
will appear lights up my soul. I have white clouds
and songs I sing at daybreak. Perhaps you touch me,
perhaps you colour the horizon as I sing.

It's like this: foals fly through life, cracks show
in the roads, winter bears a silent grudge
and spring is silently lit with lightning.
Poppies in my hands I am close to the stars.
Stroke me under the chin, brush off all my sourness
birds are flying from my brow!

Then I shook the trees, the sun grew so large,
leaves lay down to sleep and time curled up.
Flame-maned animals passed through my pulse.
I set myself up in a place morning forgot.
The stream met with the desert under a careless moon.
Wet your handkerchief and place it on my forehead.
The memories of roses and violets will shrink into shade.
Lend your breath to that memory so that mountains
linger and play, and after the mountains, me too!

translated by Caroline Stockford

Freedom

Take me away from here, I've seen so many things
I've seen so deep, so far. Long, long have I been saddened.
The time has come for mountain springs, for winds blowing
over the harvest and for the

Time for the endlessness of my shaking legs
heading towards the horizon as day opens its great door
Comprehend me from my root, not from my branch
Understand me from my dream, not from the life I've lived
Maybe the mirror is in pieces
Know me by my laugh, not by the mirror's talk.

For so long my street's been peopled with absence
With ivy's soundless climb

Its swallow: shady, slow, and always half-way there.
Take me away from this stagnation
I've seen so much of the abyss, long, long I've stared at it
That void is just repetition.

It's time for you to say you're a bird that is wetted in rain
It's time to breathe the smell of soil, fill with it, grow with it
Know me by my love, not by my loneliness.
Comprehend me from what I long for, not by what I have lost
Understand me by my childhood, not by the present version of me.

I'm coming in search of you.

translated by Caroline Stockford

Carrying in love

The napkin smeared with lipstick
you left upon the table – I carry it,
always, in my pocket.
Your smile and just-brushed hair
I carry in my mind, the scent of you
I carry in my palm as an undying rose
the smell of your breath when we kiss hello,
I carry in my surprise.
In my anger I carry those who look at
you, walking. In my excitement
I carry the rhythm of your step
curve of your high-heeled shoe
In my dreams is the sound of your dress
as you step out and it
In my sleep I carry the lightness of you
falling on my bed
In my loneliness I carry the sound of your voice
breaking into music
Every letter of you, their tone and inflection
I carry one by one in my eyes
The meaning of your dreams I carry in my fantasies.
I carry the freshness of the water you drink
In my mouth.

translated by Caroline Stockford

I got up and walked

I got up and walked
Lifted my head to the sky
and pulled the width of its vacancy towards me.

Its hands of flowing blue shortened my stride
and I stole the scurrying and the chill of clouds.

I was alone.

I thought of myself as a shower of rain
embroiling itself with winds and their
fishtailing roar.
A rain of the colourful breath of
horizons that opens sunlit flowers
I remembered how snow falls
The relationship of shadow to existence
and a few other things.
Daybreak came following those long nights
I tried to wake up, to remember before and afterwards.
I got up and walked.

translated by Caroline Stockford

What I know of the sea

What I know of the sea is so little
yet all I want to do is swim!
Without leaning too long on reality
I'd like to view all my memories
one by one; leisurely.

I'd like to go, for example, to your dream world
where you open the window and walk
where you rise and weave
your fingers into unkempt hair.

Rains wander your face, the gentleness
of dew is in your voice.

Let each and every spring be yours!
May all mountains tire and arrive here!
Here at the place where stars have spilled you
where waters flow; the place where you say
Curl up on my lap and let birds take flight
In the place where we collected questions
such as *'what was before words?'*

What I know of love is so little!
Yet I'm constantly thinking of you!

translated by Caroline Stockford

So thirsty

I'm so thirsty.
Hours resound and I'm so thirsty.
I took layers off and said 'It's June!'
Blood proliferates and now it's nearly spring
I turn to the suns and stars
to sand grains that fill the shore
and I am so tired, worn out with all the explaining
I'm freezing, let it be June right here!
I'm still so far from fires and glowing flowers.

Suddenly I think of forests, realise that I'm so thirsty.
May this city hold me and kiss me!
Without telling a soul may it secretly breathe for me.
You are so thirsty. Take my life and hidden things.
These oars and boats are yours as the sun sets
I give them to you, so that roses that fall on sea
will turn to light and touch you.
When it was thirsty you fed love on your lap
and in your wildnerness, lessened the pain of it all
May the sun never set for you!

Touch me with the wisdom of silk
for that is when the rains shall fall, not only from clouds.
Know us both by love. I thirst for you by the breast
of the light of the moon. Rain and cloud are not enough
I'll remove myself to cry as the face of long lost friends
scratch upon my memory. I know it now, I was born
with white and black. Came into being with great and small.

These unseasoned seas, like a crazy young colt scared
of the roads. We are all apprentices, fulfilling the insight
of our teachers! If I thirst, it is for yellow roses,
for kisses I was too shy to take, for love.
For all the things I want but cannot name.
I thirst and thirst... and listen when I say:
Life, I love you so!

translated by Caroline Stockford

The translators

Sevda Akyüz is a writer, translator, editor, and instructor of English. She earned her BA in English Literature at Boğaziçi University. Her translation of Gary Snyder's book *This Present Moment* will be published in Turkish in September 2022. She is also the co-editor of *Bahçe ve Kitaplık: An Anthology of Contemporary Turkish Poetry* to be published in the USA soon.

Paula Darwish studied Turkish and Middle Eastern History at SOAS and Boğaziçi University. She is a freelance translator and professional member of the Institute of Translators and Interpreters. One of her translations was *Savaşın Çocukları* by Ahmet Yorulmaz. She is also a gigging musician and regularly performs Anatolian folk music.

Clifford Endres has lived in Turkey for 20 years and has collaborated on translating such Turkish authors as Enis Batur, Güven Turan, Gülten Akın, and Selçuk Altun. His own books include *Joannes Secundus: The Latin Love Elegy in the Renaissance* (1981), *Austin City Limits* (1987), and *Edouard Roditi ve Istanbul Avangardı* (2019).

İdil Karacadağ is a freelance translator based in Istanbul, Turkey.

Canan Maraşlıgil is a multilingual & intersectional feminist writer, artist, literary translator, performer, editor, podcaster and cultural programmes curator based in Amsterdam.

Şakir Özüdoğru is a poet, academic, writer and editor from Eskişehir, Turkey. Former editor/publisher of *Gard Poetry* magazine.

Caroline Stockford is a poet, writer, translator and human rights activist from Barmouth, North Wales. She holds an MA in the History of the Turkish Language from SOAS, London University. She runs human rights projects in Turkey for PEN Norway and is a board member of Wales PEN Cymru. Her translation of Haydar Karataş's novel *Butterfly of the Night* came out with Palewell Press in 2021.

Öykü Tekten is a poet, translator, archivist, and editor. She is also a founding member of Pinsapo, an art and publishing experience with a particular focus on work in and about translation, as well as a contributing editor and archivist with *Lost & Found: The CUNY Poetics Document Initiative*.

Acknowledgements

These poems were first published in the following collections:

Kedilerin Yazdığı İlahi (Hymns composed by cats) 2014:
You decide (Sen Düşün)
I knew it as such (Öyle Bildim)
Say I want now (Şimdi istesem)
Happy birth (İyi doğdum)
Pondering (Düşünmekle)

Yağmur Dersleri (Rain lessons) 2017:
Bingöl (Bingöl)
Frontward (Önüme doğru)
Rain lessons (Yağmur Dersleri)

Dicle'nin Günlüğü (Diary of the Tigris) 2017:
Sleepless (Uykum kaçmıştı)
No room in my mind (Sığmıyor aklıma)

Günaydın Yeryüzü (Good morning earth) 2011:
Before it's too late (Geç olmadan)
It began (Başlamış)
Thinking of you (Seni düşününce)

Bir Sabah Yürüdüm (One morning I walked) 2017:
If I cry (Ben ağlarsam)

Geldim Sana (I came to you) 2019:
I came to you (Geldim sana)
This morning (Bu sabah)
It's for this reason (Bu nedenle)
Life does not lie (Hayat yalan söylemez)
Let us not speak (Konuşmayalım)
Things that are not here (Burda neler yok)
Life is seeing the flight of a butterfly (Kelebeğin uçmasını
görmektir hayat)

Tilt (Eğim)
Feather collecting (Kuş tüyü biriktirmek)
I left you behind me (Seni geride bıraktım)
Bond (Bağ)
Perhaps you touch (Belki dokunuyorsun)
What good is reading poetry? (Şiir okumak neye yarar?)
Partial look (Eksik bakış)
Such is life (Hayat öyle)
In the beginning (Başlangıçta)
Pondering (Düşünmekle)
We are after you (Peşindeyiz)
I have my reservations (Sakıncalarım Var)

Hayattayız Nihayet (We're still alive) 2021:
Freedom (Özgürlük)
Carrying in love (Sevgide taşımak)
I got up and walked (Kalkıp yürüdüm)
What I know of the sea (Deniz bilgim şu kadarcık)
So thirsty (Çok susadım)

Some have also been published in *Trafika Europe* and *Modern Poetry in Translation*

Ilhan's responses to poets form part of a forthcoming anthology of world poets writing to Ilhan, and his poetic responses to their work.